Courage does n̶o̶t̶ a̶l̶w̶a̶y̶s̶ r̶o̶a̶r̶.

*Sometimes it is a quiet voice
at the end of the day, saying,
"I will try again tomorrow."*

Finding Joy, Simple Secrets to a Happy Life
by Mac Anderson

About the Author

In September, 2003 my life was changed forever when I learned that I had Parkinson's Disease.

The diagnosis left me terrified, numb with dread and fear. Time went by, however, and I slowly began to have a change of attitude. By the grace of God, I began to accept my condition. I started to see everything as a gift of God, including this illness. I looked for the good and the positive in life. And, I decided to spend my energy focusing on what I had, not what I lacked.

I had a strong desire to gather other people together who had a similar experience. And so "The Chosen" was conceived. The Chosen was a parish group dedicated to prayerfully reflecting on the challenges those who live with illness face, be it a short-term or a chronic condition. The participants jokingly called it the group that no one wanted to join. But as we met monthly for prayer, sharing our stories of struggle and triumph, we developed a unique and strong bond. The caring and loving relationships that were forged exist even to this day.

"The Little Book of Prayer" is divided into two parts. The first section consists of brief reflections which were written for the weekly parish bulletin. These reflections are usually based on the readings for the current Sunday and are my thoughts and reactions, as they pertained to me living with illness. In addition to Holy Scripture, I used many other resources to help me pray as I developed my own relationship with Our Lord.

The second section includes five guided meditations. This ancient form of prayer has been used in the Church for centuries. The prayers are also based on a passage from scripture. A short period of reflection follows. Then, using the gift of imagination, one puts oneself at the scene, hearing the sounds, seeing the sights, being immersed in the passage described. One listens to the stirrings of the Holy Spirit in silence and stillness. This type of prayer is powerful and a wonderful means of deepening our relationship with God.

Although the contents of the booklet were written for people with illness, they are also relevant to those in good health. They can be prayed in any order. They are meant to be prayed slowly and attentively.

I offer the booklet as a gift, hoping, praying, and believing that you, too, may come to realize life's joy, with the firm conviction that each of us is guided and protected by the One who lovingly called us into existence, who loves us beyond measure, and who created us for His Glory.

Praised be Jesus Christ, now and forever. Amen.

Margo Beth Sciarrotta

A special note of gratitude to Jim and Bernadette Mangione for their generous and enthusiastic help in making "The Little Book of Prayer" a source of hope and strength for many.

With deepest appreciation to Susan and Ted Blumenthal of Minuteman Press, Ewing, NJ for their graciousness, expertise, and unfailing kindness in the preparation of the first version of "The Little Book of Prayer."

Permission has been granted for use in this project.

- *Images have been provided through Bing; Dreamstime; iStock; Shutterstock & 123RF*
- *"Put Your Hand in the Hand" Gene Mac Lellan, Songwriter*
- *@Sony/ATV Music Publishing LLC-for non-commercial use only*
- *"Everything is Beautiful" Ray Stevens, Composer*
- *Scripture Quotations-New American Bible*

My Most Important Belief

Perhaps the single most important truth-the belief that determines how I will live my life-is the realization that God is within me. This is a grace, the gift of faith. And when I respond to this grace, I begin to act in a new way. I now trust where once I lived in fear. I love others while previously I had thought only of myself. I find power flowing freely through me where before worry bound me tightly in mind and body. Realizing that God dwells not only in me, but in each person, allows me to respond to others-regardless of their appearance or their lack of physical or emotional health-with the deepest respect, kindness, gentleness, reverence.

"...the spirit of God has made me,
the breath of the Almighty keeps me alive."
Job 33:4

SLOWNESS

The society we live in today values actions, speed, a fast pace, a "go get 'em!" attitude. But those who live with illness or even the changes that come with growing older, often find that they are physically and, perhaps, even mentally slower. This calls for an adjustment in our outlook on life. It invites us to examine on a deeper level the way we feel about ourselves, our own self-worth.

But in that very slowing down lies the gift. When we can no longer enjoy the gift of good health and that wonderful energy that health brings with it, we are forced to find meaning and purpose in our lives in a new, more realistic way. Free from the distractions that come with being busy, we have the time, the ability to focus, and even the desire to reflect on that most meaningful of questions, "Why am I here?" If we are open to the Spirit, we discover how dependent we are on God, that we truly can do nothing without God. We come to the realization that we had no say in being born. Now, with humility, we ask God to help us live out His purpose in creating us to exist in this time, in this place. And, as God answers our prayer and we follow that voice deep within our hearts, we experience God's gifts of peace and hope, freely and abundantly lavished upon us!

"Show me the path I should walk, for to you I entrust my life...
teach me to do your will, for you are my God.
May your kind spirit guide me on ground that is level."
Psalm 143:8, 10

Worry

"Put your hand in the hand of the man who stilled the water; put your hand in the hand of the man who calmed the sea." Remember these words of a popular song from many years ago? Worry can make our minds seem like a troubled sea-stormy, wind-tossed, tumultuous, frightening, churning with anxious thoughts. Worry usually involves thinking ahead about the future and events which might happen but about which we can do nothing. For people living with illness, worry is more than an uncomfortable annoyance—it is an unhealthy practice that is counter-productive to healing. The times we are worried are opportunities to remember Our Lord and recall that as he calmed the Sea of Galilee, he can also calm our turbulent minds and restore peace, serenity, balance, and harmony.

"Then he...rebuked the winds and the sea, and there was great calm."
Matthew 8:26

Transfiguration

Each of us has moments of Transfiguration, those special times when God reveals himself to us in glory, majesty, and power. We are on the mountain top as we are gifted in knowing the reality of God. These moments might be catastrophic or they might come in a gentler form, as in looking in awe at a beautiful sunset and seeing the sky ablaze with indescribable colors. It might be as we gaze at the face of a sleeping child or as we look deeply into the eyes of our beloved, knowing that we love and are profoundly loved in return.

Moments like these are treasures as we savor the closeness of God. These experiences may mean nothing to another, but they must mean something to us. For we have to come down from the mountain. And we must use the energy and strength of our experience to care for those in our everyday world. For whether in good health or ill, these special moments when God touches our very soul, call us to peaceful, joyful, and loving service in a world which sorely needs it.

"This is my beloved Son, with whom I am well pleased; listen to him."
Matthew 17:5

Listening!

Listen! God calls us to listen, to hear his Voice. His Voice is in the people, the events, the beauty that is all around us. We listen, and God speaks to us in the tender words of our spouse, in the exuberance of children, in the cries of the bereaved. Those living with illness or a handicap hear the Voice in their challenges to daily living. The Voice calls them to trust, to hope, to patience, to acceptance in every facet of their lives. Each of us is called to listen to the Voice of God within us. The empty spaces of our day can be filled with TV, cellphone, or computer. Or we can choose to fill those spaces with listening to the Voice of God-the God who is the source of our strength, our wholeness, our healing, and our total well-being. Listen attentively!

"Attend, my people, to my teaching; listen to the words of my mouth."
Psalm 78:1

I Hurt...You Hurt

All people live with some sort of illness, whether the difficulty be physical, mental, psychological, or spiritual. Each of us carries the burden of pain, guilt, isolation, or rejection in some way. The Risen Christ invites us to touch these wounds by acknowledging that they do, indeed, exist. We are then able to be open to receive the healing we need. We are also called to touch the wounds of those we encounter, perhaps with a healing smile or prayer.

"He said to Thomas, 'Put your finger here and see my hands, and bring your hand and put it into my side, and do not be unbelieving, but believe.'"
John 20:27

Everyone is Beautiful

Remember the words of an old song "Everybody's beautiful in their own way"? Each one of us is God's masterpiece. Many focus on the differences among us, whether it is age, appearance, social status, religious beliefs, ethnic background, sexual orientation. In truth, we are more alike than we are different. A way to overcome our fear and prejudice toward those who are "different" is to get to know them. Many people who live with illness experience loneliness and isolation. Take the challenge to reach out and befriend someone who has a serious illness or who is handicapped. You will not "catch" their cancer, their Parkinson's, or their emotional illness. But, perhaps, you will "catch" their indomitable spirit, their strength of will, their deep faith, or their peace in acceptance. And you will rejoice in the gift of diversity.

"...in the divine image he created him; male and female he created them...
God looked at everything he had made, and he found it very good."
Genesis 1:27, 31

Caregivers

Everyone needs to feel respected and affirmed. We each have an innate need to know that we are valued and valuable, that we are loved, and that we are lovable. People who live with illness, whether physical, mental, or even going through the natural aging process, have a very deep desire to experience acceptance—it is crucial to their self-image and, perhaps, even to their survival. Illness can rob people of physical attractiveness, mental clarity, and emotional stability. Often a spouse, a child, a volunteer, or a paid helper finds themselves taking on the role of caregiver for one who is not well. The task is not an easy one and only caretakers themselves know how deeply and how often they must drink from the fount of infinite patience, kindness, and empathy. Only they know how they cannot rely on their own strength and wisdom as they try to meet the demands of caring for another. Only they know the anger and frustration, the guilt, and fear they experience as they try, in the most loving way possible, to deal with the diminishing capabilities of their loved one, a situation over which they have little, if any, control. Those who live with illness are called to shake off preoccupation with their own battles. They need to recognize how blessed they are to have a caring person whose very presence mirrors the unconditional love of Our Savior.

"This I command you: love one another."
John 15:17

Holy Week

Holy Week offers us a time to reflect on the passion, death, and resurrection of Jesus Christ. It is a time to prayerfully consider our own journey in life, as well as our own death and resurrection. This might be a good time to renew our resolve to follow even more closely the example of Jesus. Jesus knew that his life on earth was nearly over. But even in the midst of tremendous physical, mental, and emotional suffering he still chose to love others with patience and deep compassion. Jesus offered gentleness to the weeping women on the road to Golgotha, hope to the "Good Thief," assurance that his mother would be cared for after his death. Regardless of our pain or difficulties in life, we can choose to direct our energies to ensure, as much as we are able, that other people receive the care, attention, and solace they need.

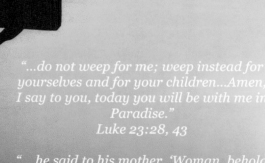

"...do not weep for me; weep instead for yourselves and for your children...Amen, I say to you, today you will be with me in Paradise."
Luke 23:28, 43

"... he said to his mother, 'Woman, behold your son.' Then he said to the disciple 'Behold your Mother.' And from that hour the disciple took her into his home."
John 19:26-27

Emmaus Walk

Who wouldn't want to walk with Jesus and hear him explain the Scriptures to them? But one way we can do this is in our own prayer. We can walk with Jesus as we quiet our bodies and minds and listen to him in silence. We can allow him to explain some of the mystery of our lives, why we are here and what we are called to do. We can also walk the Emmaus walk with another person. We can visit or connect via telephone or e-mail or invite them to share a meal. In reaching out to others, we can share our faith and truly live out this beautiful Scripture of the Emmaus walk.

"Were not our hearts burning within us while he spoke to us on the way and opened the scriptures to us?"
Luke 24:32

Accepting Help

Often we are called to listen to others speak words of faith, encouragement, affirmation to us. And we need to listen to them with an open mind and heart. We need to trust that others are sent to mirror our own goodness and capabilities. This is another gift of God-he places people in our lives who are called to serve as his voice and his eyes on this earth. So we must listen and we must respond to these invitations to see our own strengths, our capacity for wholeness and healing. Those living with illness are called to shift the focus from negativity to concentrating on what is right and good in ourselves and in our world. We also need to pray for a special blessing on those who take the time to shower us with affirmation and encouragement.

"Let your love for one another be intense...
so that in all things God may be glorified."
1 Peter 4:8, 11

Making Time For Prayer

Many religious communities gather for prayer several times during a 24-hour period. This practice is based on the Jewish tradition of praying 3 times daily. It is the ideal; those who are able to segment the day to remind themselves of God's presence are indeed fortunate.

For most of us, however, that is difficult to do. But we can tune in to the two main parts of each day, the beginning and the ending. Upon rising, regardless of the time, those who enjoy good health as well as those living with illness, might face east and breathe deeply while inviting the power, the strength, the light, and the clarity of God to come into every cell of their bodies. Seeking unity with our Creator brings wholeness and healing. In the evening we can allow ourselves to soak up the peace and calm of the quiet time as we offer thanks for the many blessings of life and of this particular day.

Praying in this way opens our entire being to the restorative power of our God.

"From the rising of the sun to its setting let the name of the Lord be praised."
Psalm 113:3

Christ Child

At Christmas we celebrate the coming of Christ as a child. Vulnerable and innocent, the Christ Child evokes a sense of tenderness, of caring, and of great love in us. We can regard those who are weakened by poor health in the same way, for they, too, are often unable to help themselves. They need our patient and gentle words, our soft touch or soothing voices, our firm arm as they struggle to arise from a chair or walk across a room. A gift we can give to those in physical, emotional, or mental decline is our attention, not fearful avoidance. As we reflect on the beauty of the Christ as child let us remember the beautiful child within each of us, and in others, that is longing to be noticed and treated with gentle love and caring.

"Let the children come to me, and do not prevent them;
for the kingdom of heaven belongs to such as these."
Matthew 19:14

Trust

Trust is a virtue to be valued. Trust is so necessary for those who deal with illness, in addition to facing the other challenges of life, in a positive and life- giving way. The much loved Psalm 23 underlines the beauty of a soul that responds to the grace of trusting our loving God. God speaks directly to us in the present, here and now. A shepherd knows that his flock are fearful, anxious creatures; he directs the sheep to a place where the water is quiet, pooling, not moving-not a river or fast flowing stream. He knows that otherwise the sheep would not drink. So, also, with us. We, although frightened and worried, are led to places of stillness, serenity, harmony, safety, and security as we respond to God's grace at this very moment. We have the promise of drinking deeply of the "still waters" and being gifted with our soul-our inmost being-renewed, refreshed, re-born.

"The Lord is my shepherd...to safe waters you lead me;
you restore my strength."
Psalm 23:1, 2

Inner Healing

While physical healing is important, often what is really needed is a healing of the inner person which may be damaged by abuse, intimidation, or neglect. In Jesus' day, women were treated as second class citizens-persons without rights who were dismissed and downtrodden. Jesus, however, treated each woman he met with respect, compassion, understanding, and kindness whether the woman was his own Holy Mother or the Canaanite woman who pestered him until he granted her request.

Motivated by devotion to Our Lady and to the women who care(d) for us, let us follow the example of Jesus. Let us resolve to become aware of and seize the opportunities to treat each woman we encounter with love and reverence. In this way, we are extending the healing touch of Jesus into a world which needs it so much today.

"Many are the women of proven worth...charm is deceptive and beauty fleeting; the woman who fears the Lord is to be praised."
Proverbs 31:29-30

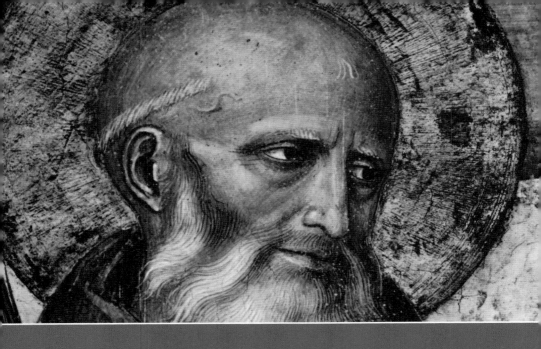

Saint Benedict

Saint Benedict in his Rule asks, "Who is the one who desires life and longs to see good days?" A resounding "I am the one!" would be expected of each of us, no matter what our situation in life. None of us knows what a new day, a new year will bring. But each day we are given the gift of a new beginning and new opportunities to respond to our life with a positive attitude. So, whether we enjoy good health or live with illness or any other loss, we are grateful for the precious gift of life. And we are able to offer not only this day, not only this year, but our whole life to God as we savor each moment of our existence. This is a way in which each of us, in spite of, or because of our individual challenges, can glorify God.

"...you...whom I have chosen and will not cast off – Fear not,
I am with you; be not dismayed; I am your God.
I will strengthen you and help you, and uphold you with my right hand..."
Isaiah 41:9-10

Dignity

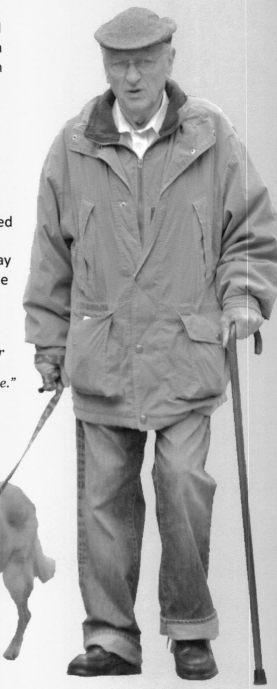

It is important to greet people who are handicapped or who live with illness in a warm and friendly manner, perhaps with a smile, a handshake, or when appropriate, an embrace. Rather than ignoring them, resolve to look past any disfigurement and focus on the person inside. Those who live with challenges to their health also have a history and a story worth telling. They need and welcome our attention, respect, and caring. In this way we affirm the dignity and value of all persons as our brothers and sisters in Christ.

"Amen, I say to you, whatever you did for one of these least brothers of mine, you did for me."
Matthew 25:40

Pebbles, Stones and Boulders

The difficulties we encounter in life can be likened to stones. Anyone who has walked with a pebble in their shoe knows that this small stone can be just as challenging as the "boulders" in life-the hurts, heartaches, losses, illnesses. The Holy Season of Easter invites us all to consider these "stones," these stumbling blocks which can deny us access to the gifts offered by the Risen Christ. Those living wth illness ask that the stones of self-pity, despair, and anger be rolled away and that Jesus, the conqueror of sin and death fill us instead with hope, joy and peace.

"On the first day of the week, Mary of Magdala came to the tomb early in the morning, while it was still dark, and saw the stone removed from the tomb."
John 20:1

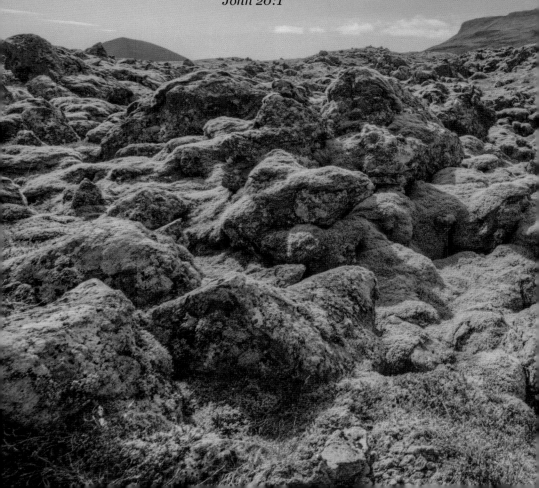

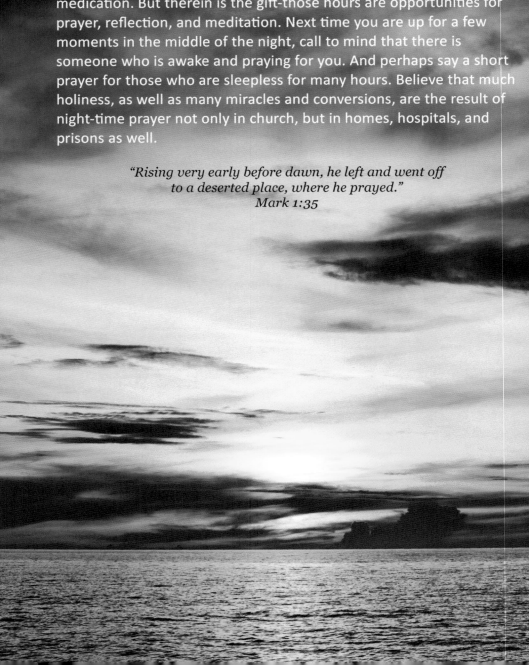

Silence, quiet, peaceful-these are some of the ways to describe the hours of night or early morning. Sometimes sleep is hard to come by for those living with illness due to changing physical conditions or medication. But therein is the gift-those hours are opportunities for prayer, reflection, and meditation. Next time you are up for a few moments in the middle of the night, call to mind that there is someone who is awake and praying for you. And perhaps say a short prayer for those who are sleepless for many hours. Believe that much holiness, as well as many miracles and conversions, are the result of night-time prayer not only in church, but in homes, hospitals, and prisons as well.

"Rising very early before dawn, he left and went off
to a deserted place, where he prayed."
Mark 1:35

Mary

Mary is a model of deep trust, an unwavering faith in God, of openness and acceptance. For anyone challenged with living with an illness, Mary gives us an example of the best way to respond to situations over which we have no control. We can choose to acknowledge that we, too, are graced and highly favored, that what happens in our lives comes with God's permission, and that in those situations we can discover the meaning and purpose of our lives. We are then able to find happiness in believing that God is with us throughout, and peace in trusting that we have all that we need to live good, holy, and serviceable lives.

"The Mighty One has done great things for me, and holy is His name."
Luke 1:49

Fear!

Fear! It is an emotion each of us feels and deals with during their lifetime. For people who live with illness, fear can be a constant and unwelcome companion. There is the worry about the outcome of the lab results or test reports, the numbness of hearing a dreaded diagnosis, the uncertainty and lack of control over our future, the terror of the lonely, all-night sleepless vigil. Our Lord understands the fear that humans experience. He lovingly compared us to sheep-gentle but jittery, nervous, frightened creatures that need a calm voice and steady master to lead them. Jesus encouraged us not to dwell on frightening thoughts when he said, "Let not your hearts be troubled nor let them be afraid." Perhaps the words of John Henry Newman, written as he dealt with his own challenges, will also offer comfort to those who struggle with fear. In his poem "Lead Kindly Light" we hear the beautiful call "Lead, Thou me on!... I do not ask to see the distant scene: one step enough for me." A healthy outlook for the ill and well alike.

"I was not ever thus, nor prayed that Thou shouldst lead me on;
I loved to choose and see my path, but now lead Thou me on!"
"Lead, Kindly Light" by John Henry Newman 1801-1890

Veronica

Veronica. Tradition has the courageous Veronica stepping out from the crowd to wipe the bloody face of Jesus on his way to be crucified at Golgotha. Veronica-giving attention, solace, and care to Jesus, who desperately needs it. For both the caregiver and the ill, Veronica has much to teach us. Sometimes all that is needed is someone who cares enough to smile, spend some time, or lend a hand. To be a modern-day Veronica is to wipe away a tear, to be aware of another's loneliness, fear, despair, or just to be present and listen. And those who are ill need to be able to graciously accept appropriate help. As we continue on our own life's journey let us recall Veronica and be more attentive to those times when we can give and receive merciful kindness.

"A large crowd of people followed Jesus, including many women who mourned and lamented him."
Luke 23:27

Patiently Waiting

Advent is a season of waiting and a time of joyful hope. Persons who live with illness are very attuned to waiting and learn to do so with patience. Prayer often fills the nights of broken sleep, calms the anticipation of the medical report, or the time before an appointment with the physician. Often this time is used for praying for loved ones, others who are ill, those in our families who are troubled, peace in the world, and many other intentions. In this way, unpleasant situations can be transformed into times of great grace for ourselves and others. Waiting becomes truly a time of joyful hope. It is another of the gifts offered to us at this time of our lives.

"May the God of hope fill you with all joy and
peace in believing, so that you may abound
in hope by the power of the holy Spirit."
Romans 15:13

Feeling Different

People living with illness often experience a sense of loneliness, isolation, a rejection that comes from being perceived as "different," not "normal," not one of "us." These thoughts and feelings can lead to a profound melancholy or depression. People need to connect with other people. This is vital to physical and mental health. Reflecting on his walk to Emmaus, we can see the wonderful example Jesus gives to us of relating to another's pain. He adopted his companions' posture and actions as he walked with them, listening attentively to their concerns, doubts, and confusion. We will have many opportunities to walk, figuratively or literally, with people who are grieving some type of loss. Let us become more and more aware of these occasions, when we accompany these special people on our journey through life. By "walking" with them, by listening to them tell of their struggles, we prepare the way for them, as Jesus did, to receive the grace of wholeness and healing.

"And it happened that while they were conversing and debating, Jesus himself drew near and walked with them."
Luke 24:15

Taking Up My Cross

The Stations of the Cross is a beautiful prayer. At the Fifth Station we reflect on a bystander who was randomly chosen from the crowd to carry the cross of Christ. Simon of Cyrene might have been reluctant at first to carry this burden. But it probably became the greatest moment in Simon's life. How Our Lord must have looked at Simon- what a moment of conversion. He literally walked with Jesus on his journey. Simon's part in this event has a familiar ring to it for those who are ill. For we, also, often struggle with bearing something difficult, something we didn't seek out. But bearing our cross with dignity and acceptance is a grace-filled opportunity to follow Jesus closely. And each of us, no matter what our situation, might do well to consider how we can help others to carry their cross.

"As they led him away they took hold of a certain Simon, a Cyrenian, who was coming in from the country; and after laying the cross on him, they made him carry it behind Jesus."
Luke 23:26

Awkward Situations

Often we do not know what to say when we encounter someone who has experienced a tragedy, such as the death of a close family member, the loss of a job, a diagnosis of a serious illness. Perhaps a resolution we can make and keep is to acknowledge another's pain and offer solace in an appropriate way. It is comforting for someone who is in this situation to be embraced, to have someone just sit with them, to hear positive words-that they are prayed for, that they are loved, that medicine is offering astounding treatments, that this must be a difficult time for them. These are some of the words and actions that help others and offer them hope, strengthen their resolve, and allow them to look inside themselves for the courage that is already there, always waiting to be discovered or renewed.

"...encourage one another..."
2 Corinthians 13:11

Who's In Control?

Probably one of the hardest things for anyone to face is a medical report that comes back with bad news. An attitude of acceptance generally comes about gradually, and with acceptance comes peace. It seems so difficult to give up control of our lives, to think that somehow our body has betrayed us. And yet, when are we really in control? All that we have is from the Almighty, starting with our very existence and the maintaining of our life on this earth. In reality, we cannot draw a breath unless God allows it. Those living with illness and those who presently enjoy good health need to be grateful for the moment and to rejoice, whatever our circumstance in life.

"Behind and before you encircle me and rest your hand upon me."

The Poor

We need not look far to find the poor, for the poor are always among us (Mark 14:7). It may seem that we only see the poor when we are in a large city, and we think it's easy to spot them. They are sleeping on the sidewalk, washing our car windows, or playing the guitar in the subway. But poverty takes many forms. We need look no further than our own family, our workplace, our neighborhood, or to the person sitting next to us in church. For who is poorer than the one who is lonely, discouraged, lacking in confidence, angry, fearful. Those living with illness are challenged in a special way to shake off self-pity and self- centeredness and to direct their empathy and energy to responding to the needs of the poor among us.

"Happy those concerned for the lowly and the poor..."
Psalm 41:1

Easter - Alleluia!

Christ is risen, Alleluia! Alleluia! And because he rose from the dead those who are ill join with all Christian people in hope and in joy. We know that one day we will be made whole-our resurrected bodies beautiful, pain-free, and radiant. But while we await our own resurrection, we rely on our compassionate Savior-who himself suffered so much-to be our strength, our shield, our rock, and our light. Praised be Jesus Christ now and forever. Amen.

"Why do you seek the living one among the dead?
He is not here, but has been raised."
Luke 24:5-6

Guided Meditations

Peter's Confession about Jesus

"Once when Jesus was praying in solitude, and the disciples were with him, he asked them, 'Who do the crowds say that I am?' They said in reply, 'John the Baptist; others, Elijah; still others, 'One of the ancient prophets has arisen.''' "Then he said to them, 'But who do you say that I am?'" Luke 9:18-20

Reflection

"But who do <u>you</u> say that I am?"

As we journey through life, at one time or another, we need to grapple with the questions "Who am I?" "Why am I here?" "Where am I going?"

In the gospel reading, Jesus asks his disciples, not only who do people say he is, but, more importantly, who do <u>the disciples</u> say he is." You see, it is important that <u>someone</u> know who we are.

It is vital for us to know who <u>we</u> really are. What is the bottom line, what is the essence of who we really are? If someone were to ask us "Who are you?" What would our answer be? We could say our name, the fact that we are a spouse, a parent. We could state our occupation, or perhaps that we're retired. We could name our ethnic background or our religion. But is that who we are at the core of our being? What would Jesus say?

Guided Meditation

During a guided meditation, we close our eyes and relax our bodies as best we can. We take a few moments to breathe deeply. If alone, simply breathe in the atmosphere. If you are with other people, breathe in the faith of the person sitting next to you. Breathe out your own faith and strength to the others in the room.

Jesus is with me here.

He is sitting right beside me.

He hears me asking myself "Who am I, Lord?" "What do I mean to you?" "Lord, how do <u>you</u> see me?"

I ask these questions very seriously. But when I look up at his face, I notice that he has a gentle smile on his face. He looks like he could give me a big bear hug and tell me not to be so concerned. But somehow he knows this is important to me. He listens as I ask him my questions. I tell him that I am so busy. I am pulled in so many directions by so many people. I need to be calm. I need to be serene. I need to think. I need to be silent. I just need to be.

And when I have finished, and only then, does Jesus look at me with tenderness and begins to speak these words:

"My precious (your name), I will tell you who I see when I look at you. I see beauty, goodness, value beyond measure. Did you not know that my Father formed you-that he knew you from all eternity, even before he made the earth and sun and moon and stars? He made you for his glory. That is the purpose of your life. That you give him praise and glory by everything you say and do.

You may be ashamed of some things you have said and done, or not said and not done. But, believe me, my Father has used everything to give glory. He has turned what was not good and transformed it into something beautiful.

Believe that the Spirit of God is within you. He is watching over you, guiding all your steps. He knows everything that you are doing, when you enter and when you leave, when you sit or stand, when you lie down and when you rise.

Before you even say a word, he knows what you will say. He knows all the longings and yearnings of your heart, all your fears and sorrows. He knows when your pillow has been wet with tears. He sees you dancing in the kitchen when you are joyful. He hears you when you sing your favorite songs.

He knows when you will die. Your time to come home is already written down in his book, so to speak. So don't worry about your death. Rather think about the good things that are happening right now. All you or anyone else has is the moment. Relish this moment and live it joyfully.

Remember that you are his child-you are a daughter/son of the Most High God, that same God who created the world and everything in it. The same God who keeps everything working precisely as it should.

His breath, his life is within you. You are wonderfully made. He knows every cell in your body. He loves you more than you could possibly know. And he wants to be close to you and give you everything you need to be at peace, to be focused, to feel infinitely loved and valued.

That, my precious child, is how God sees you. So when you look in the mirror tonight, take a good long look at your reflection. Repeat to yourself that you are good, that you are beautiful/handsome (and that you're getting better looking every day-it's true!), and that you are a daughter/son of the King of Heaven. And realize that everyone else has this dignity and value, too. And that they are to be treated also as beloved children of God.

Now Jesus takes my hand in his. He gently kisses my forehead and he is gone before I know it.

I am alone with my thoughts.

Spend the next few moments in silent prayer.

Meditation based on Isaiah, Chapter 43 and Psalm 139 (Margo's favorites)

The Woman with a Hemorrhage

...a large crowd followed him and pressed upon him. There was a woman afflicted with hemorrhages for twelve years. She had suffered greatly at the hands of many doctors and had spent all that she had. Yet she was not helped but only grew worse.

She had heard about Jesus and came up behind him in the crowd and touched his cloak. She said, "If I but touch his clothes, I shall be cured." Immediately her flow of blood dried up. She felt in her body that she was healed of her affliction. Jesus, aware at once that power had gone out from him, turned around in the crowd and asked, "Who has touched my clothes?" But his disciples said to him, "You see how the crowd is pressing upon you, and yet you ask, 'Who touched me?'" And he looked around to see who had done it.

The woman, realizing what had happened to her, approached in fear and trembling. She fell down before Jesus and told him the whole truth. He said to her, "Daughter, your faith has saved you. Go in peace and be cured of your affliction." Mark 5:24-34

Reflection

As we reflect on this gospel passage, we might wonder why the woman was on the fringe of the crowd. Why didn't she want Jesus to see her? Why did she sneak up behind him?

Other people had shouted at him to get his attention like that blind fellow from the side of the road. Or went head to head with him, obstinate in demanding his attention, like that Canaanite woman. She begged that her daughter be cured and wouldn't take "no" for an answer.

The woman with the bleeding problem in today's scripture passage had suffered so much. Anyone who has experienced this kind of problem knows how physically draining it is, how it weakens the body.

The woman was emotionally destitute and financially spent. Yet she hung back, she was timid, she was afraid to approach Jesus directly. Did she fear that being "unclean" would turn Jesus off to helping her?

She certainly was desperate. This was a last ditch try. But, fearful as she was, she did believe, she did hope, she did trust. "If only I can touch his cloak..."

How often have I experienced these same emotions, the same feelings? Sometimes I think I am not good enough, that I don't measure up, that I am not worth another's time and attention.

Living with illness, as the woman did, can make me feel "different." And there are many other situations where I seem to be "out of the loop" or set apart. I sometimes see myself as broken, "damaged goods", useless not valuable, unattractive, unproductive, weak.

And then there's my pride. Don't I think that sometimes I don't need the help that other people offer to me? "I'm okay;" "I'm really just fine"; "I can do it on my own;" "Thanks but no thanks." I tell God to give his time and attention to those who really need it. After all, he's got to take care of the planets, and the seasons, and keep all those atoms in the universe in order.

What can I matter? My worries, fears, doubts, anxieties-they all seem to shrink in importance compared to running the universe. My problems don't seem worth a glance from God.

But Jesus himself asked for help-he even asked for a cup of water that he could easily have gotten himself. And he told me that if I ask him for anything he would give it to me. He told me that he knows the number of hairs on my head. He said that he knows everything that happens, even when a little bird dies, and that I am worth much more than even that little bird.

He calmed the sea and the wind when the apostles were afraid of the storm. He offered his hand as soon as Peter felt himself sinking in the water.

He was on the lookout for those who were in turmoil-physical, emotional, spiritual. He paid attention to the short man who had to climb a tree to see him. He was respectful, even reverent, to anyone in need, to the ones that others overlooked.

I'm thinking Jesus has something to tell me. Something I need to know. Some words that meet the needs of my soul and my body. I close my eyes, settle in, and wait...

Guided Meditation

It is a beautiful day in early fall. The sun warms the daytime. The nights have been cool. It is good to open the windows to let in the refreshing night air and snuggle up in a warm bed.

But right now it is early afternoon. It is after lunch. It is quiet. I am sitting in a comfortable chair and I am just letting my thoughts come and go.

I begin to ponder the experience of the woman in the gospel passage. When was the last time I cried out in desperation to Jesus? When have I cried at night, leaving my pillow wet with my tears of hopelessness, frustration, anger?

I hear the door of this room open very quietly. And Jesus walks in. He sits in the chair next to me.

He is smiling. His eyes are kind of crinkling. He looks at me as no one else has ever looked at me. I know he loves me. Somehow he knows what is deep inside my heart. The thoughts and feelings that I have never told anyone.

I notice that he is wearing a prayer shawl. Timidly, I reach out to touch it. I wrap the tassels around my hand. I begin to speak and tell him what is in my soul.......... *(Pause)*

Jesus listens to me and nods his head from time to time. Then he leans towards me and gently holds me.

I am so at ease in his loving embrace. I listen closely in case he has something he wants to tell me... *(Pause)*

After a few moments, Jesus holds my shoulders at arm's length and looks deeply into my eyes. I close my eyes and when I open them again, Jesus is gone.

I find myself once more in this room, immersed in and surrounded by quietness, peace, and love.

Spend some time quietly praying.

Cure of the Man at the Pool of Bethesda

"...there was a feast of the Jews, and Jesus went up to Jerusalem. Now there is in Jerusalem at the Sheep Gate a pool called in Hebrew Bethesda, with five porticoes. In these lay a large number of ill, blind, lame, and crippled. One man was there who had been ill for thirty-eight years. When Jesus saw him lying there and knew that he had been ill for a long time, he said to him, 'Do you want to be well?' The sick man answered him, 'Sir, I have no one to put me into the pool when the water is stirred up; while I am on my way, someone else gets down there before me.' Jesus said to him, 'Rise, take up your mat, and walk.' Immediately the man became well, took up his mat, and walked.

...Jesus had slipped away, since there was a crowd there. ....Jesus found him in the temple area and said to him, 'Look, you are well; do not sin anymore, so that nothing worse may happen to you.'" John 5:1-9, 14

<u>*Guided Meditation*</u>

I find myself in a dark, unpleasant place.

I am near the Pool of Bethesda. I am in a sheltered spot, the place I always am. It is shady, a roof provides some shelter from the burning sun.

It is not a happy place. There are many people around me. And they are all in a bad way.

They are sick-some blind, some deaf, some with ugly sores. It stinks in this place-the awful smell of illness and decay.

And I am one of those who smell. I am dirty. My hair is greasy.

I cannot walk. I don't really know if I want to walk. I use this time to think. I think about my mother and father and what they didn't give me as a child. I get really angry at them. I wonder if it wasn't for them, maybe I wouldn't be here-I would be with those people out there.

Clean, healthy, buying something good to eat or nice to wear.

I think about being so sick and weak. I never had a chance to be somebody. I didn't have the chance to make something of my life.

I seethe with anger, the injustice of it all. I feel the rage of jealousy and hatred.

How I would like to kick and scream, if only I could.

I don't like feeling this way, but I don't know what to do about it. It seems like everything and everybody is against me.   /

I shrink down on my mat. I don't deserve to live like this. But I don't know any other way to live.

I feel almost comfortable living in squalor, defeat, and misery. I revel in it.

Do I feel sorry for myself? You bet your life I do!

The sound of someone approaching startles me out of my dark mood. I look up and see a man coming straight at me.

What does he want?

What's that he's saying? What is he asking me? "Do I want to be cured?"

I don't know what to say. I am tongue-tied. What kind of a question is that?

I can hear my own whining voice as I begin to complain that I have no one to put me in the waters when they are moving. So I lose out every time. The story of my life.

But then I look up and see the way he's looking at me.

I see those eyes. They look straight through me. He KNOWS!

He knows what is in my heart-all the despair, all those black thoughts, all the hatred, all the loneliness.

I am still as he gazes at me. I feel my heart melting.

Then he tells me to pick up my mat. And he tells me to walk.

And I do just that. I can hardly believe it!

But I just can't leave this place I've lived in so long. I wander around. I see the wretched-ness around me in a new way. My heart softens as I see people suffering.

All of a sudden I see him again-the one who told me to pick up my mat and walk. He says something strange. But I know what he means. He tells me to sin no more or something worse will happen to me.

I know that I was full of hatred and anger. But now my heart is being cured, too. I walk out into the sunshine, with my mat under my arm, praising God.

Questions for Reflection

What is my "mat?" What am I carrying around with me that weighs me down? What burdens do I live with?

Do I really want to be cured? What do I need to be cured from?

Is it easier for me to whine and complain than to admit my faults? Can I hear the voice of Our Lord Jesus gently calling me out of the squalor I live in to a place of beauty and peace? Will I say "yes, Lord" to Him?"

**Spend some time quietly praying.**

The Raising of the Widow's Son

"...he journeyed to a city called Nain, and his disciples and a large crowd accompanied him. As he drew near to the gate of the city, a man who had died was being carried out, the only son of his mother, and she was a widow. A large crowd from the city was with her. When the Lord saw her, he was moved with pity for her and said to her, "Do not weep." He stepped forward and touched the coffin; at this the bearers halted, and he said, "Young man, I tell you, arise!" The dead man sat up and began to speak, and Jesus gave him to his mother."
Luke 7:11-17

Guided Meditation

It is a cool, rainy day.

The sky is gray and overcast with thick clouds.

This weather is unusual for this time of the year in Israel.

But the gloominess matches the mood of the great crowd of people I am with. My friend is here numb with grief.

Her son is being buried today.

When he was but a baby, we walked with her here as she buried her young husband.

But she had her son and he grew to be a fine young man.

He cared for his mother. There was a deep and tender love between son and mother.

And then all too soon, he too, was taken from her. And so we walk this sorrowful walk with her. Suddenly, there is a commotion.

Someone is saying that Jesus is passing through this city. He has his group of followers with him.

I notice him as he sees the funeral moving slowly by.

His eyes seek out the weeping mother. His face softens as he approaches her.

Someone has told him about this widow.

Jesus reaches out his hand slowly and gently touches the coffin. I cannot believe my eyes! I cannot believe my ears!

He tells the young man to get up. And then the son begins to speak. I cannot hear the exact words but suddenly the son is with his mother.

The crowd is frightened. I am afraid. What kind of man is this who brings life where there was only death?

I go off by myself, but I am not alone. Jesus is here with me. He sees that I am troubled. I see his face, so gentle, so kind, so knowing. I begin to tell him my fears, my worries, my concerns. I tell him everything.

(Pause)

As I look up at him, I see only love and mercy and acceptance. Jesus tells me these special words and I listen carefully.

(Pause)

As softly and as quickly as he came, he now leaves. But, not really. For I can feel his presence with me.

I feel stronger, energized, focused. My heart aches with love for anyone who is suffering.

Spend a few moments praying in silence.

Questions for Reflection

Is there a time in your life when you have experienced the healing touch of God?

Who or what has brought you back to life?

Jesus calls all of us to be the gift of life for someone. How can I be the touch, the word, the one who raises another to life?

The Man with the Withered Hand

"Moving on from there, he went into their synagogue. And behold, there was a man there who had a withered hand. They questioned him, "Is it lawful to cure on the sabbath?" so that they might accuse him. He said to them, "Which one of you who has a sheep that falls into a pit on the sabbath will not take hold of it and lift it out? How much more valuable a person is than a sheep. So it is lawful to do good on the sabbath." Then He said to the man, "Stretch out your hand." He stretched it out, and it was restored as sound as the other. But the Pharisees went out and took counsel against him to put him to death."
Matthew 12:9-13

Guided Meditation

It is a cool evening in Jerusalem. It is the holy Sabbath.

I am in the temple, just one of many in this crowded place.

It is getting dark and the shadows are lengthening.

I find a place near a large column where I can see, but few can see me.

Suddenly, I hear a commotion. There is a lot of loud talking and finger pointing. People are looking at a young man who has entered the temple. It is Jesus, the new prophet and miracle worker that everyone is talking about. There is a following of some men and women with him.

Our leaders approach him. There is an air of authority in them as they walk towards Jesus.

I can't hear what they're saying, but I notice that Jesus is looking over the crowd.

He beckons the man standing next to me to come to him.

The man hesitates. But then he goes forward and stands in front of Jesus. There is a slight breeze blowing. And I notice that one of the sleeves of the man's tunic seems empty. But wait-it's not empty.

As the sleeve of the tunic blows aside, I can see a dark form—a hand. It is spindly and shriveled.

It looks so fragile, like a twig that someone could break just by stepping on it.

Jesus regards the man with an understanding and knowing look. I can tell that Jesus knows how much the man has suffered because of his condition. The rejection, teasing, embarrassment he has experienced. The humiliation of being limited in the work he can do.

Then Jesus touches the man's withered hand. And, all at once, the blackened, useless flesh is a healthy color.

The hand is firm and whole, strong and healthy.

The man is jubilant. And I, too, am so amazed at what I have seen that I pay no attention to the elders.

But, then, I look up to see Jesus looking directly at me. How could he notice me? I have been standing in the shadows.

He beckons for me to come to him. I look around, hoping he means for someone else to approach him.

But there is something about him which draws me to him, and I slowly walk to where He is waiting for me so patiently.

At first, I do not look at him. But when I do look up, I see the gentlest and kindest of faces. Jesus looks at me with a slight smile on his face. His eyes are twinkling.

I feel as though He can see into my very soul.

He begins to speak to me. He invites me to reply. I am reluctant at first. But it is as though there are only the two of us.

He listens to me intently, nodding his head as I am speaking. He then asks me what I would like him to do for me.

I look into his eyes. I see compassion and understanding. I have the feeling that he knows what I am going to say even before I utter a word.

But I begin to tell him what I need, what I would like him to do for me. (Pause) When I have finished, He gently pulls me aside so that we can sit down together.

He then begins to speak to me. He says... *(Pause)*

I lower my eyes for a moment, overwhelmed by his presence. And when I look up again, he is gone and I am once again alone.

But, I am not lonely. I can feel his sweet presence still with me. I can feel deep within me a sense of peace and contentment.

Questions for Reflection

What is in my life that seems withered, dry, useless to me?

What am I ashamed of? What do I keep hidden from others?

Am I willing to "stretch out" what is painful for me to live with and receive healing?

Spend some time quietly praying.

Made in the USA
Columbia, SC
05 January 2018